D1260801

PAMPHLETS ON AMERICAN WRITERS • NUMBER 63

UNIVERSITY OF MINNESOTA

William D. Howells

BY WILLIAM M. GIBSON

UNIVERSITY OF MINNESOTA PRESS • MINNEAPOLIS

Printed in the United States of America at
the North Central Publishing Co., St. Paul

Library of Congress Catalog Card Number: 67-26663

PUBLISHED IN GREAT BRITAIN, INDIA, AND PAKISTAN BY THE OXFORD
UNIVERSITY PRESS, LONDON, BOMBAY, AND KARACHI, AND IN CANADA
BY THE COPP CLARK PUBLISHING CO. LIMITED, TORONTO

WILLIAM D. HOWELLS

WILLIAM M. GIBSON has compiled a Howells bibliography with George Arms and has edited the Mark Twain–Howells letters with Henry Nash Smith. He is a professor of English at New York University and director of the Modern Language Association Center for Editions of American Authors.

William D. Howells

As a journalist, poet, travel writer, critic, and novelist, W. D. Howells wrote professionally for nearly seventy years. In 1852, when *The Blithedale Romance* appeared, Howells at the age of fifteen published his first poem; he was still writing a column for *Harper's* in the year of his death, 1920, when *Main Street* burst upon the literary world. Achieving editorial power and a name before he was thirty, he came to know, or to interpret, justly on the whole, every American writer of four generations, the forgotten Melville excepted. He introduced to American readers a host of Continental novelists, at first noticing their fiction in the French, Italian, and Spanish editions. He was the first advocate and editor and became the warm friend of Henry James and Mark Twain. For forty years he made his literary convictions strongly felt, first as editor-reviewer and then as conductor of critical departments in influential magazines.

From 1875 to 1895 he was at his most imaginative and productive. His work earned the praise of Turgenev, Tolstoi, Taine, Verga, Hardy, Shaw, and Kipling. At the same time, certain English reviewers attacked Howells for maligning Dickens and Thackeray while lesser American critics accused him of vulgarity and lack of idealism. Ambrose Bierce sneered at "Miss Nancy Howells and Miss Nancy James" for their gentility. But the effect of this criticism on the reading public was negligible. Howells's fiction and travel volumes continued throughout these years to sell steadily (if never spectacularly). By the turn of the century, however, the tide had shifted. Thereafter, his creative power waning, he was still often praised but less frequently read. As the "Dean of

American Letters," he became in effect a dean without faculty or students. Late in life he noted wryly his loss of popularity, saying his statues were cut down, "the grass growing over them in the pale moonlight."

Then, when Mencken in 1919 charged that Howells "has nothing to say"; when Van Wyck Brooks a year later persuaded many readers, even Sherwood Anderson, that Howells had clipped Mark Twain's wings by censorship – Lewis Mumford renewing the charge; and when Sinclair Lewis on winning the Nobel Prize in 1930 identified Howells with "Victorian" restrictive codes, Howells had reached the limbo of being subject rather than object. Certain readers might take pleasure in D. G. Cooke's and O. W. Firkins' critical studies (1922, 1924), or find the letters edited by his daughter Mildred (1928) full of life and intelligence. But the bright spirits of the second American literary renaissance took Mencken and Lewis and especially Brooks at their word. Beyond the usual American whirligig of taste, one reason for their revulsion seems clear. These leaders in a decade dominated by Freudian doctrine were chiefly familiar with Howells's latest, least vigorous writing. Determined to break through the literary conventions governing sexual morality of earlier decades – conventions which they identified with Howells – they convicted Howells of prudery and optimism and condemned him forthwith.

The depression years of the 1930's saw Howells regain some of his lost stature. As Fitzgerald vanished and Steinbeck appeared, the liberal and radical critics, dismayed and protesting, looked to the American past for present comfort and rediscovered Howells as a Christian socialist. In the succeeding decades a group of scholar-critics have further redressed the balance. His life has been well outlined, his best novels have been distinguished from the worst and partially explicated. But his boldness and subtlety as a critic are scarcely recognized even now, and the full breadth and depth of his work need to be understood. To that end the reader must bring something like Howells's own sensibility—an appreciation of irony, social comedy, and style, and a taste for both James and Twain, Jane Austen and Tolstoi, Emily Dickinson and Thorstein Veblen. Howells's "beautiful time," as James envisioned it, and a just valuation of his work are yet to come.

In the meanwhile a new reading of Howells's life, encompassing yet going beyond Edwin H. Cady's solid, full, pioneer biography, ought to be made, and certain of its emphases may be suggested here. One obvious justification for such a new reading is that sketches of his life before Cady's were rendered impossibly gray by adulation, indifference, or ignorance. Another reason, challenging in nature, is that Howells, though willing enough to write of literary acquaintance and literary passions, spoke of his own life infrequently and guardedly. "Cursed with self-consciousness to the core," he hated, he said, to write of his early life "because it's so damned humiliating." His mood of reserve is curiously like Melville's or Hawthorne's when late in life he told Twain: "I'd like immensely to read your autobiography. You always rather bewildered me by your veracity, and I fancy you may tell the truth about yourself. But *all* of it? The black truth, which we all know of ourselves in our hearts, or only the whity-brown truth of the pericardium, or the nice, whitened truth of the shirtfront? Even you won't tell the black heart's-truth. The man who would do it would be famed to the last day the sun shone on." The inner life, in short, of "William Dean Howells"—he disliked his full name heartily—and its intellectual and emotional crises remain only half explored.

Howells began life with a difference. His boyhood and early manhood in post-frontier Ohio (1837–60), typical in many respects, were still such as to make him both proud and self-conscious about the differences between his family and their neighbors in the villages of Hamilton and Jefferson. Jefferson was no more a cultural waste for a lively printer's apprentice, it is true, than the Hannibal, Missouri, of Sam Clemens, "Mark Twain." But the complex of circumstance and temperament was already marking young Howells with inchoate desires for life in city-centers of culture such as Columbus, Boston, or New York, for experience of the countries of Heine and Cervantes, and for literary fame. Unable to recall a time when he could not set type, the boy grew up with hard work and poverty in a large and close-knit family whose goal was to own a printing plant, a newspaper, and a home. His earliest neighbors had been largely southerners, yet even after the family moved to northern Ohio, their antislavery, Quaker, and Swedenborgian principles set them and him off from others. The backwoods communal experiment which his father and uncle undertook for a year in the country, near Xenia, at "New Leaf Mills," was unusual, if not unique. Other boys shared many of his childhood fears, but few or none of his young friends suffered until marriage and maturity from a private "demon" created by fears of hydrophobia, the ghosts of contemporary spiritualism, the world's coming to an end, and early death. These fears culminated in a recurrent nightmare of fire and alarmed cries of "Arms, Poe, Arms, Poe," induced by his reading of *Tales of the Grotesque and Arabesque*; eventually, in Howells's mid-teens, they led to hypochondria and nervous breakdown. William C. Howells's reassuring his son that he too had suffered from fears when young afforded some release; the rest came for Howells in constant reading, venturing into the classical languages, studying German, Spanish, and French, and writing poetry.

How much of Howells's later writing is fitfully illuminated by his childhood! His portrayal of ineffectual, warmhearted characters, with a touch of Colonel Sellers, like his father. His profound distrust of the Puritan tradition and Quaker dislike of violence, comparable to Whitman's. His ineradicable memories of hard work and bone-deep fatigue balanced against strong contempt for the scrambling life of self-made men. His lifelong preoccupation with communal experiments and with dream analysis. His devotion to principle in the face of popular disapproval. His taste for the "cleanly respectabilities." And withal, his establishing a pantheon of culture heroes and cultivating from the beginning the humors and ironies of Cervantes and Heine.

When Howells became news and literary editor of the *Ohio State Journal* at Columbus (1857–61), he began to breathe the air of a larger world, in spite of bouts of homesickness. Dickens, Tennyson, and the New England poets joined the pantheon of Heine, Cervantes, Goldsmith, and Shakespeare. James Russell Lowell accepted five of his poems for the *Atlantic* for 1860. He published *Poems of Two Friends* with J. J. Piatt, presumably thinking of Wordsworth and Coleridge. He wrote a good campaign biography of Lincoln. And he danced and talked literature and made friends and courted a visiting New England girl, Elinor Mead, in the deep-lawned homes of the state capital's simple, open society. The royalties from his campaign biography and a contract for newspaper letters made possible a pilgrimage through Canada to eastern publishing centers. In Boston, Lowell introduced him by letter to Hawthorne, and he met Holmes, Emerson, and Thoreau as well. In New York he encountered the *Saturday Press* Bohemians and Walt Whitman at Pfaff's beer parlor. A year after his return to Ohio, his biography and his family's political devotion won for him a long-hoped-for opportunity, a position as American consul in Venice. A familiar cycle in American letters was once again to repeat itself.

The four years in Venice (1861–65), which included his marriage to Elinor Mead in Paris and the birth of Winifred, their first child, in Venice, completed an education begun at the type case in Hamilton, Ohio. Witty, loquacious, something of a bluestocking, talented in art and letters, this girl from an idiosyncratic Vermont family remains a shadow in Howells's biography. Yet in these first years of marriage, Howells was liberated from the fears and the provinciality of his youth and he acquired professional skills as a writer. Though it remains largely undefined, Elinor Howells's influence upon her husband was subtle and strong, and along with his rich experience of Italian life and letters, it prepared him for the central role he would play for over four decades in American literature. Passing a turning point in his life, he had discovered that his gift was analysis of character, both national and individual, in simple, finely wrought prose. He had read Italian history, Dante, contemporary poetry and drama, and he had immersed himself in the stream of vulgar Italian life. Above all he had read (and witnessed in the Teatro Malibran) the plays of Carlo Goldoni and the *commedia dell'arte* which reflected the same life. Thus, having translated Goldoni's memoirs (published in 1877) and produced fresh travel sketches and criticism, the slender, diffident journalist came home stouter and stronger in his craft, an Italianate American.

But it was not to Ohio that Howells returned, for American publishing centers were in the East. Acutely aware that he might be trailing behind in the post-Civil War procession, Howells fell back on literary journalism in New York City for a temporary "basis" and a livelihood. Writing free-lance reviews and editorials quickly led to his conducting a department, "Minor Topics," for E. L. Godkin's *Nation*, and in his column he turned easily from reviews of Dickens, Whitman, and the Longfellow translation of Dante to murder, scandal, divorce, criminal insanity, New York politics, defense of the liberated Negro, the consular service, and the troubles of the Fenian brotherhood.

Boston was still his goal, nonetheless, and when in 1866 James T. Fields, Lowell's successor, offered him the assistant editorship of the *Atlantic,* Howells fulfilled the dream of his mature life (as he then thought), conceived when he first visited New England before the war. Though not officially editor-in-chief until 1871, Howells was soon actually in charge and responsible for a change in character in this avant-garde monthly. Over a fifteen-year period, he made it a national magazine, accepting contributions from the South and the West, introducing new features (music, political comment), and favoring a fresh, colloquial style. He met deadlines, read proof closely, wrote lead reviews, searched out new talent, and made many friends and certain enemies as he rose in these years from the status of minor poet and skilled journalist to that of new novelist and nationally known editor.

Perhaps the chief effects upon Howells of the editorial burden and of established editorial policies were delay in his development as a writer of fiction and limitation, in a degree, of what he might choose to represent in his fiction. The great success of *Venetian Life* (1866), a book which he had fashioned from his travel letters to the *Boston Advertiser,* and of *Italian Journeys* (1867) persuaded him to apply his skill in observing Italian characters and manners to the American scene. But *Atlantic* subscribers demanded reserve in the treatment of love and courtship in the pages of the magazine, and Howells therefore had to fit his treatment of sexual mores, in his first stories and novels, to *Atlantic* conventions. "Scene," for example, which depicts a Boston prostitute's suicide by drowning, is the only one of the *Suburban Sketches* which did not first appear in the magazine. Similarly, Howells could not easily forget that his approving Harriet Beecher Stowe's essay in defense of Lady Byron and Fields's publishing it lost the *Atlantic* some thousands of subscribers. Yet another consequence of Howells's editorship was his tendency to overvalue certain of the founders of the *Atlantic*: he had read them in the West, and now they made him – almost – one of them. He knew Emerson and Thoreau and Hawthorne chiefly in their work, and their work encouraged him in the direction of his own talents. But his adulation of Lowell, Longfellow, and Holmes was for many years restrictive and even stultifying, as his reaction to Mark Twain's speech burlesquing the New England worthies at a birthday dinner for Whittier suggests – clearly he overreacted.

If editing the *Atlantic* cramped Howells's talent in certain respects, however, it freed it in others, for the audience was intelligent and critical; certainly it made possible the flowering of other writers' genius. In the postwar years, Howells met Henry James, Jr., in Cambridge, published his early stories, and talked with him about the art of fiction for hours on end. Subsequently he competed with James for subjects, and with him invented the "American girl" and the international novel; he placed James's late novels; and he elucidated James's fiction discriminatingly for four decades. Howells's friendship with Mark Twain, which was even closer, was of prime consequence. It began with his praise of *Innocents Abroad* (1869) in the *Atlantic* – an act comparably free and bold with Emerson's letter praising Whitman in that Howells was approving in print a "subscription book," that is, vulgar "non-literature." Thereafter Howells guided Clemens, so far as a friend and editor might, away from burlesque and failures in *vraisemblance* and mere buffoonery in the direction of his true capacities: an entire spectrum of satire, humor ranging from black to bright, true pathos touched with the tears of things, speech in the mouth, epic action, and living characterization. Howells was the first and most sensitive of Twain's critics, who never touched his copy when it was right and who was midwife to most of the work by which Twain is now known.

Finally, despite the restraining influence of the "countinghouse" and the limited sensibilities of feminine readers, Howells was able to use his editorial power on the *Atlantic* to extend the horizons of American fiction by selecting what to publish and by the great weight attached to his reviews. He gave short shrift to sentimental-domestic-melodramatic tales, and devoted his attention to stories that were autochthonous in setting and probable in action, whose characters possessed "God-given complexity of motive." Thus, early in his editorial career, he detected realistic traits and qualities in certain novels of Elizabeth Stoddard, Bayard Taylor, and Henry Ward Beecher, but praised with greater enthusiasm the work of Björnson, George Eliot, and J. W. De Forest as he discovered it. Later, he discovered realism full-blown in the dramatic method and the sensibility of Ivan Turgenev, the directness and humor of Mark Twain, and the analytic subtlety and moral discrimination of James. And he drew upon each of these three masters as he wrote his own fiction at the time.

During his last years as editor of the *Atlantic,* Howells grew "miserably tired of editing" and correspondingly eager to write plays and fiction full time. The breaking up of the firm of Houghton and Osgood, which had published the *Atlantic,* a severe illness, and Winifred Howells's nervous prostration led him to resign the editorship in 1881 and take his wife and children abroad again for a year. Howells reached the peak of his power as a novelist in the decade that followed and as a critic took the leading role in a violent intercontinental war over realism. In the decade he wrote his best dramatic and international novels, *A Modern Instance* and *Indian Summer*; the transitional novel *The Rise of Silas Lapham*; and the major novels of social criticism *Annie Kilburn* and *A Hazard of New Fortunes.* In it he wrote telling criticism of the comparative and rhetorical kind, much of it in "The Editor's Study" column of *Harper's,* on Tolstoi, Dostoevski, Zola, Verga, Galdós, Hardy, James, and Twain. In it too he suffered a painful revolution in his mode of thinking and feeling, a revulsion from self and self-interest comparable to the "vastation" that Henry James, Sr., had undergone more than forty years earlier.

The change began, probably, in his growing uneasiness over the widening social and economic chasm in America, and in his reading of Tolstoi and the American socialists Gronlund, George, and Bellamy. The change grew at a bound when he chose deliberately to risk his career and livelihood by declaring publicly that the Chicago anarchists, in 1887, had been unfairly tried – this from the writer who sought to be regarded as he himself regarded Cervantes. His altered viewpoint made his success taste of ashes. Then, when his daughter Winifred died, after a long, obscure illness, it deepened to the conviction that personal happiness can bear no part in the legitimate goals of a man's life. James had written of Winifred, "To be young and gentle, and do no harm, and pay for it as if it were a crime" – and Howells added, "That is the whole history of our dear girl's life." Howells's last major move, from Boston to New York and a new publisher, Harper and Brothers, took place in these years and has traditionally marked this profound change in his life. The change was scarcely unique: *The Princess Casamassima, A Connecticut Yankee,* and *Looking Backward* attest to the same deep unease. But Howells's "vastation" has not yet been fully understood in its nature and its consequences.

After 1892 as a novelist Howells entered upon a plateau inclining gradually downward. *A Hazard of New Fortunes* was followed by many novels on a smaller scale, but only two of them, *The Landlord at Lion's Head* and *The Leatherwood God,* are of comparable quality. The social criticism becomes direct and overt in a series of articles, or is imperfectly integrated into the Altrurian romances. More significantly, Howells began his series of literary recollections and reminiscences, and after a time returned to literary journalism. Yet his practical criticism of this period, of plays and fiction, is distinguished, and his lecture on "Novel-Writing and Novel-Reading" represents his critical theory at its comprehensive and penetrating best. The criticism becomes less tendentious than it was in "The Editor's Study," is extraordinarily sensitive to the currents of impressionism and naturalism among new writers, and treats the mature realists' work in a deeper perspective. Between ages fifty-five and sixty-five Howells first revealed the special qualities, lesser and greater, of Emily Dickinson, Crane, Garland, Fuller, Frederic, Norris, and Veblen, and of Herne, Harrigan, Ibsen, and Shaw. At the same time, novelists so different as Dreiser and Kate Chopin were reading and profiting from his fiction. Howells was also working, at the century's turn, to syndicate in newspapers the work of a group of novelists, including James, and to gain for them a wider audience and larger royalties; but he had to give up the scheme when he found that its backer was a former book pirate. He largely failed, as well, opposing national policy in the Philippine phase of the Spanish-American War. Even so, his anti-imperialist rhetoric, like that of Mark Twain and William James, is vigorous and memorable.

Until his death at eighty-three, Howells continued to review books and events in the "Editor's Easy Chair" of *Harper's*. He still wrote well when he was stirred by Ibsen or Brand Whitlock or Wells or Zola or Havelock Ellis, or the Irish executions in 1916, and he was still open to such new works as the poetry of Frost, Masters, and Lindsay and the *Education of Henry Adams*. The autobiographical *Years of My Youth* (1916), and *My Mark Twain* (1910), which Edmund Wilson calls the "best character" of Twain we have, bear comparison with the best earlier writings. Howells took keen pleasure in a variety of activities in his green old age: in serving as the first and continuing president of the

American Academy of Arts and Letters and in preventing the Academy from accepting endowments; in cultivating his garden at Kittery Point, Maine; in talking about the movies with his admirer and denigrator, Sinclair Lewis. He was writing about Henry James when he died.

Cooper, Melville, and Mark Twain wrote their first novels on a bet or at the urging of friends, turning from active lives to the writer's study. Hawthorne, Emily Dickinson, and James on the other hand became engaged in the craft of literature at an early age, and Howells is one with them in this matter of conscious literary intention. His first ambition was to become a lyric and narrative poet like Longfellow, sustaining himself by literary journalism until poetry would support him. But the popular failure of *Poems of Two Friends* (1860) and of *No Love Lost, a Romance of Travel* (1869) became the "turning point" of Howells's life, as he later explained, especially in the light of the high critical success of *Venetian Life* (1866). In this new kind of travel book, the first of many, Howells had contrasted the high art and the deep past of Venice with people and incidents in the shabby-picturesque present. The point of view is distinctly American, the tone is ironic in the manner of Heine, the style is finished. His "fatal gift of observation" already apparent, the young ex-consul and *Atlantic* editor turned to fiction.

From "The Independent Candidate, a Story of Today" (1854–55, never collected) to *The Leatherwood God* (1916) Howells wrote thirty-five novels – and more than forty tales and sketches. Apart from the juvenile "Candidate" story, *Suburban Sketches* (1871) is Howells's first tentative venture into fiction. With an eye educated by the Italian experience, Howells drew Irish and Italian and Negro figures in the Cambridge background, and expanded his scenes from the serving girl at home and doorstep acquaintance, through horsecar vignettes, to Boston and Nahant. Two scenes, however, are very largely imagined. The first depicts recovering from the Charles River the body of a drowned prostitute, the second an ex-convict's "romantic" yarns about his past. "If the public will stand this," Howells wrote to James, "I shall consider my fortune made." The public response was favorable, and Howells took a long step toward the novel in his next book.

"I wrote 'Their Wedding Journey,'" Howells remarked to an interviewer long afterward, "without intending to make it a piece of fiction. . . . It was simply a book of American travel, which I hoped to make attractive by a sugar coating of romance." Howells's distrust of his "fitness for a sustained or involved narration," however – he admitted it in the first page of his book – was quickly dissipated. A family friend whom he had asked to mark passages embodying real incidents marked instead "passages which were purely invention," and Howells was elated: he had proved his fictive art. He was also gratified when the first edition of 1500 copies sold out in a day.

The biographical elements in *Their Wedding Journey* (1872) are apparent in Howells's letters of the time and in the manuscript. Howells framed his narrative on his summer's travel with his wife, in 1870, from Boston to New York and Albany, Buffalo, Montreal, and Quebec. He also used descriptive bits and thumbnail character sketches which he had already printed in the travel columns written for Ohio newspapers in 1860, when he had made his literary pilgrimage to New England by way of Canada. Within this framework, nonetheless, *Their Wedding Journey* is fiction. Rapidly limned characters encountered along the route come to life as Basil and Isabel March, delayed honeymooners, talk with them and react to them. The Marches, in fact, provide such action as there is by humorous persiflage and frequent clashes of opinion and occasional quarreling. They also lend depth to the travelogue by recalling Francis Parkman's interpretations of the French-Canadian past, and by comparing Canadian to European sights. Howells provided a rationale for his story thus: "As in literature the true artist will shun the use even of real events if they are of an improbable character, so the sincere observer of man will not desire to look upon his heroic or occasional phases, but will seek him in his habitual moods of vacancy and tiresomeness." More positively, Howells has March tell his wife the story of Sam Patch, who invented the saying "Some things can be done as well as others" and tested it by jumping over Niagara Falls twice. From this tall tale, March then infers that Americans will never have a poetry of their own "till we get over this absurd reluctance from facts . . . till we consent to face the music in our simple common names, and put Smith into a lyric and Jones into a tragedy." *Their Wedding Journey,* which Henry Adams called "a pleasing and faithful picture of American existence," thus exemplifies Howells's early, anti-romantic, Emersonian theory of realism, a tradition that led to Eugene O'Neill's *The Emperor Jones.*

The Saguenay-Quebec travel scene again forms the background for *A Chance Acquaintance* (1873) – "There's nothing like having railroads and steamboats transact your plot for you," said Howells to a friend in 1871. But Kitty Ellison, who had appeared briefly in *Their Wedding Journey,* is a real creation. She is a girl from the West, brought up to revere John Brown and the abolitionists of Boston, bright and witty and unconventional, with natural good manners and taste. She finds the Canadian scene and character as rich and strange as Miles Arbuton of Boston thinks them dull, especially by comparison with European counterparts. Howells probably found his idea for the clash of such differing temperaments in Jane Austen, but his characterization is original – and so is his conclusion. Kitty in the end rejects Arbuton's suit, wholly in accord with Howells and James's shared determination, at this time, to avoid the "everlasting young man and young woman" as a subject for serious fiction. Howells's satire, moreover, on one kind of Boston manners – the stiffness, coldness, and extreme self-regard of Arbuton – is pointed and amusing. James considered Kitty too pert, in the early serial chapters, and also wondered whether Arbuton's proposal might not have been dramatically rendered. But, he wrote his friend, he delighted in a figure "so real and complete, so true and charming." It is no wonder, for Kitty is the older sister of James's Daisy Miller, the first fictional portrait of "the American girl" who would make for Howells and James a linked reputation.

Howells's first "true novel," *A Foregone Conclusion* (1875), was also his first international novel. He was now prepared to venture beyond Canadian-American or native East-West contrasts, and by juxtaposing characters of the New World in the Old, to dramatize a tragic *donnée*. "The hero is a Venetian priest in love with an American girl," he wrote James. "There's richness!" The idea for the novel he had presumably been recurring to since 1866, when he thought of beginning "a romance – the scene of it to be laid in Italy, or Venice, rather" and composed an editorial for the *New York Times* on the celibacy of the priesthood as a cause of corruption in Italian society. He argued further that the current advocacy for clerical marriages was "the most natural and consequent growth from present conditions." Howells drew certain touches in the career of his skeptical inventor-priest from the life of Padre Libera, with whom he had read Dante a decade earlier, and introduced his friend Padre Giacomo, of the Armenian convent, very briefly as Padre Girolamo, a character who serves as a foil to Don Ippolito. But these, along with details of setting repeated from *Venetian Life*, are borrowings at the surface. *The Tragedy of Don Ippolito*, as Howells first titled the novel, gains its depth from four fully imagined characters, a tragic action that develops from their relationships, and a highly functional setting.

In the development of his American consul, Ferris, Howells breathes life into the anti-romantic convention that people rarely fall in love at first sight: for all his intelligence, Ferris is inwardly diffident and slow to recognize that he has become jealous of Don Ippolito, a priest. Howells's Mrs. Vervain, the wealthy widow of a choleric American army officer, is as addlepated as she is amiable. She is thus unable to perceive that Don Ippolito is falling in love with her daughter while he tutors her in Italian, and she is even capable of leading the young priest to believe that he might make his way in the then dis-United States. The moody seventeen-year-old "heroine," Florida Vervain, wavers between sharp-tongued outbursts and remorseful self-abasement. After humiliating Don Ippolito, she promises misguidedly to help him leave the church in which he has never truly believed and find a career in America as an inventor. With these three portraits, Howells's grasp of character matured. But the relationship of the Americans, all of them types of innocence, to the dreamy Italian cleric who has turned his oratory into a forge marks an even greater advance of the novelist in his craft, for it is Don Ippolito's character and the breakup of his illusions that count most. Into this figure Howells dissolves faint aromas of Don Quixote, of Arthur Dimmesdale, of Shylock, in order to show him a divided man, inwardly tormented by "a black and deadly lie." Don Ippolito is both unbelieving priest and impractical inventor, "under sentence of death to the natural ties between himself and the human race" and increasingly deluded in the belief that Florida may love him. Howells had thus firmly prepared his actors, his entangling action, and his setting for the climactic chapter. In the moonlit, walled garden of Casa Vervain, the priest declares his love to Florida, who first repels him in unconscious shock and distaste—and then embraces him in pity and understanding before she runs out of his presence. The unobtrusive symbolism and symbolic reference made in earlier chapters now reach their height simultaneously, as the garden fountain that Don Ippolito had repaired to run briefly every day from its limited supply of water, "capering and babbling on," "all at once, now, as a flame flashes up and then expires . . . leaped and dropped extinct at the foot of the statue."

Howells marred the perfect verity of this ending, under pressure from James T. Fields, by adding a foreshortened epilogue in which he shifted his setting, reported the death of Don Ippolito, and concluded with the marriage of Florida to Ferris. "If I had been perfectly my own master . . ." Howells admitted to C. E. Norton, "the story would have ended with Don Ippolito's rejection." As it was, he kept the final action credible and somber enough. Ferris and Florida speculate fleetingly about Don Ippolito's feelings and motives; and in their consciousness finally he "ceased to be even the memory of a man with a passionate love and a mortal sorrow."

Howells's development as a novelist cannot always be neatly periodized. After completing a major work, he frequently lapsed into an earlier accustomed manner before venturing further—or continued to satisfy the taste of his public for psychologized tales of courtship. So, although it comes after *A Modern Instance* (1882) and *The Rise of Silas Lapham* (1885), both works of more scope, *Indian Summer* (1886) may be said to culminate Howells's first period of small-scale novels of manners, and is probably the best of them. Two interim works preceding *Indian Summer* are "Private Theatricals" (*Atlantic,* 1875) and *The Lady of the Aroostook* (1879). The first is a brilliant comic account of Belle Farrell's destroying the friendship of two young men who both become her suitors. A master of feminine psychology, Howells surpassed himself in delineating Mrs. Farrell, a New England Hedda Gabler before Ibsen. Like De Forest's Mrs. LaRue, she is beautiful and clever and irresponsible and yet somehow sympathetic, because she is driven by passions she does not fully understand. The second is a once very popular but much slighter work. In Howells's own words, it is the story of a girl, who, by a series of misunderstandings, "finds herself the only woman on board a vessel going to Italy with three young men" who "do everything they can to keep her from embarrassment or even consciousness," one of whom marries her when they get to Venice.

Howells took especial pleasure in writing *Indian Summer,* chiefly because the realistic comedy of manners (one surmises) was the form most congenial to his temperament in his first period. The story grew out of his revisiting Italy in 1882–83 with his family, and duplicates certain pictures and episodes from Florentine history in *Tuscan Cities* (1886), a travel book that overlapped the novel in serial parts. The runaway carriage episode, the artist Inglehart (Duveneck), and the wish of the point-of-view character, Colville, to write a cultural history of Florence stem from Howells's recent direct experience. Understanding of the pervasive tone of the novel, however, its color and flavor, must be sought in his ambivalent attitude toward Italy revisited and in his response to the values of melancholy and nostalgia in Turgenev's fiction. The sense of loss was all the more clearly defined for him by the rapturous encounter of his daughter Winifred, then eighteen, with the country of her birth.

Indian Summer, Howells told Mark Twain, "is all a variation on the one theme" of January and May, of youth and age. The variations are amusing and complex. Effie Bowen, whom De Forest considered "the most perfectly painted child in fiction," appears to be twelve. Her mother, Lina Bowen, is a charming widow of thirty-eight. Imogene Graham, their guest in Italy, twenty, a happier Florida Vervain, is counterpointed against mother and daughter. And the forty-one-year-old Colville, involving himself with all three, creates discords among them and multiplies the bemuddlement and the humor before final harmony is attained. Two memorable "confidants" help to spin the plot and clarify the theme. Elderly, curious Mrs. Amsden is always one stage behind in tracing the changes within the triangle and thus maintains the comic note. The Reverend Mr. Waters, aged seventy, who has cheerfully left Haddam East Village for Florence, forever, considers Mrs. Bowen and Colville young and provides Howells perspective.

The narrative method of *Indian Summer* is dramatic. The mood is nostalgia for lost youthful love and the Italian past, in the manner of Turgenev, well tempered by irony and wit. The characters, as noted, are Americans in Italy, of all ages. The action is single, culminating in Colville's marriage to Mrs. Bowen, after his engagement to the girl, Imogene, breaks of its own sentimental weight. But Howells's transforming into fictional life his leading ideas – that longing for youth when youth is past results only in the waste of human energy and devotion, and that the notion of self-sacrifice may prove a pure mischief – is achieved only by close attention to motive and characterization. When Imogene strikes youthful attitudes, or confides her delusions to her astonishing diary, or teeters happily at the edge of a mismarriage, she errs foolishly and openly. Mrs. Bowen's faults are more subtly, though quite as clearly, indicated. The older woman's repressed jealousy and her wish to conform to European codes of behavior lead her to bewilder Colville and to torture Imogene and herself. Colville, though he often acts like a proto-Prufrock, is a paragon of common sense compared to the women of the novel. As for the carriage accident that reveals Colville's love for Mrs. Bowen, or Effie's appeal at the last moment to prevent Colville's leaving, these are acceptable *coups de théâtre*, because Colville now recognizes Imogene's immaturity, and Imogene has weighed Colville's social ineptitudes and found him wanting. The tone is high comedy. Only the dullest reader would expect disaster in *Indian Summer*.

Colville's sentimental dream of recapturing his lost love, reembodied in Imogene, thus ends happily in the "clear light of common day" and an uncommonly happy marriage. Colville's inner conflict, however, the tug of war within him between American present and European past, remains unresolved, to profounder but equally satisfying effect. Howells's skill as a novelist is well displayed in the natural symbolism by which he represents this wavering equilibrium. At key points in the action, scene, and internal dialogue, he enriches the theme of Indian summer by contrasts in age, in weather, in season, in history, in country. To name only three: When Colville first glances out on the piazza where he is lodging, it seems full of snow, until he discovers that "it was the white Italian moonlight." Further, Howells manages a most delicate and natural allegory of Florentine flowers to illuminate Colville's varying relations with Effie, Imogene, and Mrs. Bowen – the flowers he gives or forgets to give and the flowers they prefer. (The reference is as unforced in *Indian Summer* as it is exotic and artificial, for example, in Melville's *Mardi*.) And again, at Etruscan Fiesole, the mild Italian spring and the ancient landscape with "history written all over it" are set in Colville's consciousness against the raw country around Buffalo, New York, bursting impatient and lavish with "blossoms and flowers and young leaves and birds." In short, *Indian Summer* embodies the international theme in high comedy, and Colville is an earlier, more fortunate Lewis Lambert Strether. On finishing the work, Howells consciously abandoned the international field to James, and turned his full attention to the American scene.

In Howells's first period, therefore, he began by adapting his formula of travel and observation to fiction, with the sanction of the picaresque novel and perhaps of Heine's *Pictures of Travel.* The methods of Hawthorne and Turgenev and maturing concepts of motive and character led to the comedies of manners and courtship—with the Howellsian difference. Toward the end of the period Howells considered himself a "built-in novelist" because he was competent to begin serializing a work before he had finished it. Yet, despite increasing intensity in plot, the early books are alike in their depending on intersectional and international clash and contrast and on dramatic encounter between "two persons only, or three or four at the most."

In the second period, 1880–86, Howells turned to the American scene and to certain large problems of contemporary life. His characters increased in number and variety; his novels grew longer, from six to eight or ten magazine installments. He found justification first in Zola and then in Tolstoi for his matter and his motives. Most strikingly, he had come to the decision to excise those humorous or reflective comments on which he had heretofore leaned heavily in order to win approval for a character or an action—asides which formed for many readers a signature of his style and manner. Thus, the manner of Goldsmith or Thackeray or Heine is much diminished in *A Foregone Conclusion,* and by the time of *Indian Summer,* it has either vanished or become an element of the speech of Colville, a created character.

The second period opens with *The Undiscovered Country* (1880), "a serious work" Howells called it, which ventures into an area that he would explore again and again: the channels into which the will to believe was flowing in contemporary America, as religious convictions decayed and religious sanctions weakened. In this novel Howells sets the delusions of spiritualism in New England against Shaker belief and practice. Dr. Boynton's long decline as a spiritualist parallels the growing liberation of his daughter and medium, Egeria, and reaches its climax in his discovery that his spiritualism has been only a grosser kind of materialism. Apart from its intrinsic interest and its treatment of the father-daughter relation, the novel forms an interesting link between Hawthorne's *Blithedale Romance* and James's *The Bostonians.*

Dr. Breen's Practice (1881) also explores the growing feminist mood of the decade, but the author's stance is at least as masculine and satirical as it is sympathetic. Though Dr. Grace Breen, a homeopathist fresh from medical school, is first humbled by and then humbles the allopathist Dr. Mulbridge, her marriage to the man she loves cannot alter her bottom nature. She is a belated Puritan, a devotee of New England "dutiolatry."

A Modern Instance (1882) is a very different story. It was born in Howells's mind as "The New Medea" when he conceived an Indiana divorce case as a commonplace example of the dire ancient conflict in Euripides' drama. It grew with Howells's experience of the quarrels between his summer landlord and landlady in 1875 and 1876 – a "tragedy, dreary and squalid beyond conception," he called it. It was written under the stimulus of reading Zola, "everything . . . I can get my hands on," and displayed a powerful motive and a firm grasp of the characters. Ostensibly the novel treats divorce and the failure of belief; less obviously but more truly it probes the mystery of love turned to hatred.

Marcia Gaylord is a most intensely imagined and realized character – pretty, self-centered, full-blooded, bewildered, hotly jealous. She is the child of parents who are as attached to her as they are cold to each other. Her marriage to Bartley Hubbard ends disastrously, partly because her uncontrolled temper and tendency to self-indulgence find counter-traits in her good-humored but amoral husband. Squire Gaylord, the agnostic lawyer of

Equity, Maine, and his reproachful self-effacing wife habitually allow Marcia her way but do not give her a sustaining standard of conduct or belief. Hubbard, an orphan who has made his own way through college into small-town journalism, achieves his majority like Marcia with few convictions and grows increasingly sure that only those of his acts that the world sees can be of any account. Given a chance at the bar, enough money, a few friends, Hubbard might have prospered and lived out his life, however stormily, with his wife and child – so Howells seems to imply. But the virus of countinghouse journalism and Marcia's loss of faith in him lead to his cheating Kinney, a devoted friend, for money. This using of a friend brings on, in turn, the break with Ricker, his friend and conscience, the losing of his editorial job, and a final violent quarrel with Marcia over his encounter with a former Equity girl turned prostitute. When Hubbard leaves Boston and loses his pocketbook, return seems impossible. He perjures himself seeking an Indiana divorce, again runs away when confronted in court by the enraged Squire Gaylord, and dies – so it is reported – in Whited Sepulchre, Arizona.

James's well-known charge that the American scene too meagerly nourished the novelist's needs is refuted in this novel. As Howells wrote his publisher, J. R. Osgood, his story was to be on "no mean scale geographically." He was fully aware how the background, East and West, might add life to his characters and clarify his theme. So tight-fisted Equity, where the rats smell in the wainscoting, prefigures Boston as the Hubbards know it, a city of high rents and mean streets and sharp social cleavages, and the raw town of easy divorce, Tecumseh, Indiana, as well.

The Tecumseh courthouse and its tobacco-chewing idlers form the backdrop for Howells's most intense scene. There Squire Gaylord, accipitrine in feature and in his hatred of Bartley, defends his daughter's conduct and proves his son-in-law a liar, only to be brought down in the midst of the trial with a stroke. Howells does not end *A Modern Instance* at this point, however. True to his realistic tenets he returns to half-crippled Ben Halleck's futile struggle between his conscience and his long-indulged love for the widowed Marcia, and to the debate, still further removed from reality, of Clara Kingsbury and her wealthy lawyer-husband, Atherton, as to Ben's proper course. But the issue is no issue. Bartley is dead. Halleck regresses to Calvinist orthodoxy and self-punishment. In Marcia the spring of tenderness is broken, and she will, surely, return to the narrow life of Equity and "stiffen into the old man's aridity." Though the ending of the novel is open, it is not indeterminate.

When *A Modern Instance* appeared, Robert Louis Stevenson (who had married a divorcée) withdrew an invitation to Howells to visit him because he thought Howells was condemning divorce. Much later Edith Wharton accused Howells of "moral timidity" that had checked him from arriving at a logical conclusion, even as she acknowledged his pioneer treatment of "the tragic potentialities of life in the drab American small town." Neither writer had followed the long logic of the tale or understood Howells's view that "the novel ends well that ends faithfully." No second marriage could ever redeem the past for either Halleck or Marcia Hubbard. Despite the weakened dramatic tension in the last chapters, Howells achieved his "strongest" work, as he himself believed, in *A Modern Instance*. It is a moving representation of moral ignorance and moral decay, unmatched until Dreiser imagined Hurstwood and Fitzgerald created Dr. Diver.

The Rise of Silas Lapham (1885) opens dramatically with an interview between Bartley Hubbard, still a struggling reporter, and the newly rich paint-king of Boston, on the perennially fascinating subject of how he had made his million. The novel has always been popular, partly because it presents Lapham's financial and social failure as "consciously and deliberately chosen" when he has to decide whether he shall cheat and stay on top in business, or tell the truth and fail irrecoverably. Lapham's true rise is therefore moral, and all the more dramatic in the context of the elastic business codes of the Gilded Age and his own business failure.

How much the novelist had learned of his art by the age of forty-eight appears in the complexities of the plot. Lapham's physical strength and bulk and country speech indicate that he is still the son of a hard-scrabble Vermont farmer. He is vigorous, raw, naive, uneducated, and socially ambitious for his wife and two daughters – a man who had risen fast as a competent soldier and officer in the Civil War. In sharp contrast, Bromfield Corey is physically slight, well-educated, once fought under Garibaldi and has lived much abroad, lives moderately on family money, and plays at painting. In wit and ancestry he represents the Boston Brahmin type par excellence. Howells's device for bringing the two families into contact and conflict is chiefly the confused triangle of Tom Corey, the son, and Irene and Penelope Lapham, the daughters. Tom's polite attention to both girls and Irene's charming but nitwit egotism lead the Laphams to believe that he loves Irene, so that Tom's eventual proposal to witty, reserved Penelope precipitates a period of harsh learning of "the economy of pain," as the Reverend Mr. Sewell calls it, before Tom and Penelope marry – and leave for Mexico.

But the heart motive of the novel, as Howells's original synopsis shows, is Lapham's determination to emulate Boston society and to make his family a part of it. The first clear sign that he will fail occurs in the dinner party scene at the Coreys', midway in the novel, when Lapham becomes boastfully tipsy – the result of his being unused to wine and of Corey's lapse of tact as he fails to note this fact. The vividest symbolic indication of Lapham's determination is Silas's "letting out" his mare and cutter one winter afternoon on the Longwood road. Driving with iron control and unmolested by the mounted policemen, he passes a "hundred rival sledges" with little apparent risk. The effective symbol of Lapham's desire is his building a new house on the Back Bay – a handsome, airy structure, with library and music room, to be decorated in white and gold. It is the product of an architect's taste, chiefly: Lapham contributes only money. The impression of this new house is strengthened by contrast to the ugly farmhouse of Lapham's childhood; the dark, overheated, overfinished house in Nankeen Square; Mrs. Corey's "old-fashioned" house with a classic portico and "bare" interior; and Bromfield Corey's "ancestral halls" in Salem, presumably of the seventeenth century. When the new house burns to the ground, the insurance on it lapsed, Lapham must confess that he had set it on fire himself, carelessly, trying out his new fireplace. In the end, Lapham wrestles, like Jacob, with an angel and achieves an unhappy victory with his conscience; he tells Sewell that if "the thing was to do over again, right in the same way, I guess I should have to do it." Howells presents the larger conflict of Laphams and Coreys more stringently, however, and despite the marriage of the most businesslike Corey and the most cultured Lapham, the couple cannot remain in Boston. Of this conflict, Howells says: "It is certain that our manners and customs go for more in life than our qualities. The price that we pay for civilisation is the fine yet impassable differentiation of these. Perhaps we pay too much; but it will not be possible to persuade those who have the difference in their favour that this is so."

The Rise of Silas Lapham is more finely proportioned at the beginning than in the last third. This may be due to Howells's need to foreshorten Lapham's slow business decline; but it also stems from his inability to make business loss as interesting as social climbing, or even as Irene's error in love and her hardening into maturity. James's comment on his *Roderick Hudson,* that its head was too big for its body, applies equally here. But in terms of style, the novel deserves its reputation. Bromfield Corey's wit and Penelope's tartness gain from contrast with Colonel Lapham's boastful speech, in the idioms and rhythms of his New England vernacular. Howells's narrative prose is equally functional, concrete, and clear. This was the style that both James and Twain, themselves stylists, found so distinctive and took so much pleasure in.

The serious motive and the large impression of occupations and professions that Howells sought in the fiction of his second period gave way to profound concern with social and economic questions in the third period, the decade from 1887 to 1894. In these years he suffered his profound spiritual and psychological crisis. The ground shifted under his feet when he stood, almost alone, in a glare of publicity after he asserted the rights of the Chicago anarchists. His daughter's death brought sharp suffering: perhaps he had sought the wrong treatment. He experienced a sense of alienation, as well as excitement, in moving to New York. In 1886, almost inadvertently he became involved in a sharp, often bad-tempered, running battle concerning the new realism with a host of critics because of his "monthly ministrations of gall and wormwood" in "The Editor's Study" of *Harper's.*

Howells plunged into this storm of change, weathered it, and emerged from it largely by learning the "transcendent vision" of Leo Tolstoi and adopting Christian socialism. Most of his novels in the period have been characterized as "economic" novels, and it is true that they share certain characteristics of the *tendenzromansk* or propaganda novel, a form Howells scorned. Ideologically they culminate in *A Traveler from Altruria* (1894), a Utopian romance that brings together Howells's ideas in defense of liberty, equality, and fraternity in that altruistic "other land" which America only partially shadowed forth. But "novels of complicity" is a more accurate tag than "economic" novels, because complicity is the dominant concept in them; and a "panoramic theory of fiction" – Howells's own phrase as Van Wyck Brooks later reported it – is equally useful since it fits these works concerned with the lives of many rather than few characters. These definitions, however, apply only to the main stream in the third period; they will not account for *April Hopes* (1888) or *The Shadow of a Dream* (1890) – both substantial novels and each different in form and motive.

In *The Minister's Charge or The Apprenticeship of Lemuel Barker* (1887) Howells first fully stated his doctrine of complicity, combining it with that major motif of the nineteenth-century novel, the provincial in the city. The minister, Sewell, has unintentionally encouraged Lemuel to come to Boston from his home in the country by politely dishonest praise of the boy's poems. Lemuel becomes his "charge." And in a sermon he is driven to conclude that "no one for good or for evil, for sorrow or joy, for sickness or health, stood apart from his fellows, but each was bound to the highest and the lowest by ties that centred in the hand of God. . . . If a community was corrupt, if an age was immoral, it was not because of the vicious, but the virtuous who fancied themselves indifferent spectators." Sewell's rhetoric is heightened by echoes from the marriage ceremony, and takes on additional ironic force in the context of Barker's fortunate escape later from marriage to a factory worker, "poor, sick, flimsy little Statira" Dudley. The reason for Barker's escape is striking. Just as sexual passion turning to hatred and the persistent tie between father and daughter had spun the plot of *A Modern Instance*, so masculine, "whopper-jawed" 'Manda Grier retains her hold, implicitly sexual, upon Statira, against Barker's sense of obligation to the girl. Thus "The Country Boy in Boston" – this was Howells's first title for the novel – fails and returns to the country; and thus Howells stands the American drama of the self-made man on its head. The work is suffused with other and subtler ironies that delighted Mark Twain, for example, which make up for the blurred double focus on Sewell and Barker. To suggest only two: Sewell preaches complicity but is unable to conceive of Barker's torment when he falls in love with the gentle Jessie Carver while he is still pledged to Statira. (One thinks of Clyde Griffiths.) The society girl Sibyl Vane treats Barker as her inferior with cutting arrogance, even as she finds time to bestow "a jacqueminot rosebud on a Chinaman dying of cancer" in a charity hospital.

The naked issue of charity versus justice becomes, in fact, the central issue of *Annie Kilburn* (1889), though Howells keeps his actors in this Tolstoian novel thoroughly limited and human. For all his social passion, Peck, the egalitarian minister of Hatboro, Massachusetts, cares little for his motherless child. Putney, the lawyer who defends the mill workers in labor disputes, is a periodic drunkard. And Annie Kilburn, Lady Bountiful with a conscience, fails utterly in her efforts to help the working poor of her company town, marries the apolitical doctor, and "waits, and mostly forgets, and is mostly happy."

Between March 1889 and October 1891, Howells published in serial form three extraordinary books: *A Hazard of New Fortunes* (1890), *The Shadow of a Dream* (1890), and *An Imperative Duty* (1892). The third is an intensely imagined study of miscegenation. The second, taking its title from *The Scarlet Letter*, explores the morbid psychology of jealous delusion; it is an experimental novel rendered from three points of view, anticipating rather than following James. The first is very simply Howells's biggest novel. It sets forth panoramically, as *Manhattan Transfer* would later, the struggles of fifteen major characters and a host of minor figures to establish a national magazine in New York City and to enter into its "vast, gay, shapeless life." The execution of the Chicago anarchists and the Brooklyn trolley-car strike of 1889 provided Howells with a "strenuous action" and an "impressive catastrophe." A "moment of great psychological import" both national and private added tensions. And his theme, the American scramble for success with the inner revulsions bred by that struggle, lent the whole fable "dignity," as Howells himself later claimed.

A Hazard of New Fortunes envisions the city as a magnet and a microcosm. In social terms it contrasts Margaret Vance, the sensitive girl of old New York society, with the Dryfoos daughters, Christine and Mela, whose one aim is to break into society under the guidance of the well-paid Mrs. Mandel. The elegant but unsure Beaton wavers in the middle, courting independent Alma Leighton and flirtatious Christine. At the bottom are Lindau and a prostitute pursued by the police, slum-dwellers, the one by choice and the other by necessity. In political-economic terms, the novel presents Dryfoos as the coldest of newly rich entrepreneur-speculators, with Fulkerson as his prophet, in contrast to Conrad Dryfoos, the son, who turns from his father and his father's life to passive resistance and Christian socialism. Similarly, Colonel Woodburn, whose private integrity matches his admiration for the feudal institutions of the prewar South, is set against Lindau, a German revolutionary who has lost his forearm fighting slavery in the Civil War. Still another kind of contrast appears in the characters' attitudes toward art: Beaton's great talent, Alma Leighton's aspirations, the barbarous taste of the Dryfoos family. In moral worth as well, Howells sets his characters in a kind of hierarchy, as George Arms has argued, from lowest to highest: Beaton, Dryfoos, Fulkerson, March, Woodburn, Lindau, and Conrad Dryfoos.

The measure of Howells's skill in representing "God-given complexity of motive" within these characters is that they act out their roles credibly. Beaton fails in a half-comic attempt at suicide. Lindau, a new John Brown, fights with the police in the strike and, his arm again shattered, dies of injuries. Conrad attempts conciliation in the strike and is shot in the heart. Dryfoos suffers, and takes his half-savage daughters off to Europe. Margaret Vance becomes a nun in a charitable sisterhood. March, the witness and chorus-character, is now able to buy the magazine that originally brought the group together. Yet at the moment of his success, March says to his wife, ". . . so we go on, pushing and pulling, climbing and crawling, thrusting aside and trampling underfoot; lying, cheating, stealing . . . to a palace of our own, or the poorhouse," blind to the principle that "if a man will work he shall both rest and eat." "And so we go on," March cries, "trembling before Dryfooses and living in gimcrackeries."

Howells had looked at Boston society from the bottom in *The Minister's Charge.* He had surveyed a Massachusetts mill town from the top in *Annie Kilburn.* Now in *A Hazard* he consciously employed the "historical" form, anatomizing New York City through many eyes. Though James thought the "composition" weak, he found the novel as a whole "simply prodigious," just as Twain considered it "a great book" wrought with "high art." One may not dismiss these appraisals as friendly prejudice: the novel singularly combines the wit of Jane Austen and the elaborate irony of Thorstein Veblen, before Veblen. It is a broad, vital comedy, as provocative in its implications as it is entertaining in its fable, in which Howells artfully and unobtrusively colored the public dream of success with private awareness of complicity.

Following the period of novels of complicity, which ended in the romance *A Traveler from Altruria,* Howells reverted to smaller canvases in his fiction, now persuaded that the great social questions must be represented from within rather than from without. Characteristic and perhaps best of the novels between 1894 and 1908 is *The Landlord at Lion's Head* (1897). Here Howells's idea was to bring a true New England rustic type into conflict with Cambridge and Harvard society, and his bottom motive was to realize "that anti-Puritan quality which was always vexing the heart of Puritanism." The great ambition of his hero, Jeff Durgin, is to build a fashionable summer hotel on the shoulder of his native mountain, Lion's Head. In the course of realizing it, the aggressive Durgin hardens from the contempt he suffers as a "jay" at college, and from his experience with three young women. Genevieve Vostrand refuses Jeff's offer of marriage, preferring a titled Italian, but at the last after separation from her husband and her husband's death, accepts the successful "landlord." Bessie Lynde, a Cambridge society girl, flirts and has a tentative affair with Jeff before her alcoholic brother horsewhips him. Cynthia, the country girl with whom he has grown up, who loves him, is reluctantly forced to give him up. With all three girls, but especially with Bessie, Jeff gets a dark glimpse into "the innate enmity between the sexes" in the game of courtship and passion – "passion lived" and "passion played." As the novel ends, Durgin is thoroughly successful on his own terms, taking for his motto, "You pay, or you don't pay, just as it happens." His career has borne him out. He might have succumbed to drink, except for his will and his constitution. He might have formed a dangerous liaison with Bessie Lynde, but her brother whipped him. He might have murdered Alan Lynde, but circumstance and obscure impulse spared him. He might have committed arson and been caught, but the old hotel burned by accident. Clearly, Howells created this new Bartley Hubbard, the successful failure who suffers from an incapacity for good, with special sympathy and entire aesthetic control. More nearly naturalistic than any other story by Howells, it is as Delmar Cooke judged it "a master novel."

Finally, *The Leatherwood God* (1916) represents a late, fine flowering of Howells's talent and his one punitive tragedy. It re-creates the rise of an actual Ohio backwoodsman of the 1840's, who deluded others and even himself momentarily into believing that he was God. Dylks's power arises from his stallion-like sexuality and from the will to believe of spiritually starved women of the frontier. His fall is necessary, but it is moving because it carries so many with him.

Turning from Howells's fiction to his critical theory, one may observe that interpretation of his fiction is further advanced than elucidation of his critical principles or his practical criticism in their full range. Three reasons for this condition may be suggested. First, the mass of Howells's critical writing remains uncollected and it is therefore difficult to view it in sequence or as a whole. Second, Howells's usual critical stance implies that criticism is a secondary form of discourse. Third, the body of critical writing by which he has usually been judged, *Criticism and Fiction* (1891), is argumentative, rhetorical, for the moment, and not wholly representative. It is well to recall that the novel came to be treated seriously, as "literature," only within Howells's lifetime, and that much contemporary criticism was vitiated by irresponsible anonymity or puffery or exhibitionism or ignorance. Howells wrote reviews and critical essays in every year from 1859 to 1920, as a journalist. But he loved literary art, especially the art of fiction. His best criticism is reasoned, reflected, distilled. He was a critic in spite of himself.

Despite his low opinion of the critical office, then, Howells formed a theory of fiction that was subtler and more eclectic than literary history has allowed. Certainly its effect was and has been far-reaching. (It is possible that he is one of those masters "who are more accepted through those they have influenced than in themselves," but this is not the view taken here.) Hackwork and journalism aside, few critics of his day are comparable to him in breadth, in subtlety when he is engaged, and in clairvoyance.

The first element, at once apparent, in Howells's early theory of the realistic novel is his dislike for "*Slop, Silly Slop*," as Nanny Corey characterizes a popular novel. The generic sloppiness of such fiction, Howells believed, derived from sentimental thought, melodramatic action, and poorly motivated character. Of course, James, Twain, De Forest, and many lesser realists shared Howells's revulsion and strengthened him in his view. Very early, Howells and James decided to ignore or play down, so far as they could, simple-minded courtships in favor of other significant relations — of mother and son, father and daughter, husband and wife — and of other passions than love, such as avarice, ambition, hatred, envy, devotion, friendship.

Conversely, Howells early developed a positive concept of form from the example of Turgenev and by reaction against the method of his early idols, Dickens and Thackeray. If readers were to take the novel seriously, then the novelist himself must take his craft seriously, and without intruding or commenting or appealing to the reader, learn to represent, to describe, and to dramatize. That is, if the illusion of life was worth creating, it was worth preserving unbroken. "Everything necessary to the reader's intelligence should be quietly and artfully supplied," Howells maintains, "and nothing else should be added." In these early years Howells distrusted the French writers for the moral vacuity or the obsessive sexuality in their tales, but he accepted as law Flaubert's dictum that the writer must be everywhere present in his work and everywhere invisible. A corollary of this dramatic ideal of Howells was that a strong motive and a firm, long-brooded-over grasp of character were equally necessary for the aspiring realist. It was character that counted, and not the "moving accidents" and thrilling adventures of earlier or popular contemporary tale-telling. In short, Howells's first concept of the novel was that the writer ought to begin by imagining several characters in the round, then bring them together to work out a credible dramatic action. He accepted the ideal of the novel of character the more readily because biography and autobiography fascinated him, both their form and their matter, and he was already writing and translating plays. Howells stated this double principle clearly in his essay on "Henry James, Jr.," in the *Century* (1882).

Plot, then, in the sense of continual gross or overt actions, Howells found less interesting than the slower pace of life as he observed it, "interiorly" and "exteriorly." It followed that a novel might end inconclusively, in the view of readers accustomed to the usual marriages, prosperity, and tying up of loose ends, and yet end faithfully and "well." Howells's youthful passion for Cervantes, his fondness for the episodic "memoirs" of Tom Sawyer and Huckleberry Finn, and his pleasure in the moral logic of Isabel Archer's final decision all confirmed him in his approving the open or ironic ending. To cite only one example, from his fictional practice, he brought *April Hopes,* a sardonic story of courtship, to this conclusion: "If he had been different she would not have asked him to be frank and open; if she had been different, he might have been frank and open. This was the beginning of their married life."

As the vehicle for the "new fiction," Howells advocated, published, and practiced a new, supple, colloquial English, taking as his authority writers so diverse as Dante and Emerson, James Russell Lowell and Artemus Ward, Mark Twain and Henry James. The "language of the street" in many regional varieties functions vitally in his own fiction, and he praised it as it appeared in the "local color" stories of Harte, De Forest, Cable, Frederic, Garland, and even Norris and Crane. He even taught it with some success to his Norwegian protégé, H. H. Boyesen. Mark Twain chiefly created a revolution in the language of fiction; Howells was the architect of the revolution. For many years Howells effectively and persistently advocated the use in fiction of native backgrounds, manners, and speech, often in the light of national difference. Hence it is no wonder that he pioneered, with James, in the international novel, and invented a new kind of city-novel. H. L. Mencken, who cites Howells frequently in *The American Language*, brackets him only a little grudgingly with Twain and Whitman as a chief proponent of American English. Thus, the language line from Emerson through Howells, Twain, and Whitman to Stephen Crane, Robert Frost, Gertrude Stein, Sherwood Anderson, and Ernest Hemingway is a line of direct descent.

These, in sum, are the major propositions of Howells's earlier theory of fiction, and most of them persist in his later theory. He modified his views in several respects during the free-lance years, 1881–86, and the period of novels of complicity and argumentative criticism, 1886–94. Most obviously, he wrote panoramic novels with larger casts of characters under a compulsion to treat the "social question" in an economic chance-world. A less apparent but equally significant change was his creating chorus characters, to serve as centers of consciousness or to focus upon ethical issues implicit in the action. Atherton, Evans, Sewell, the March couple, and others create the illusion of an ongoing society by their reappearance; but their prime reason for being is to debate moral questions more lucidly than less conscious or less dispassionate characters can. But, despite the success of *A Hazard of New Fortunes*, Howells never lost his interest in the psychological "novelette." Both *The Shadow of a Dream* (1890) and his liking for Stephen Crane's economical, effective stories suggest this persisting interest. In fact, Howells came in the end to believe that "the phenomena of our enormous enterprise" were not truly the "best material for fiction," except as such wonders of the "outer world" could be related to the "miracles of the inner world."

Defining Howells's key terms, especially as they are used in his later essays on major writers and in his lecture "Novel-Writing and Novel-Reading" (delivered 1899, published 1958), will serve to round out this sketch of his fictional theory, and to suggest his view of the ends of literature. Howells conceived of three ways of representing life in fiction: the novel, the romance, and the romanticistic novel. The novel, which comes from the sincere endeavor "to picture life just as it is," deals with character and incidents that "grow out of character." It is the "supreme form" of fiction, exemplified in *Pride and Prejudice, Middlemarch, Anna Karenina, Fathers and Sons, Doña Perfecta,* and *Marta y María.* The romance, Howells says, deals with life "allegorically," in terms of the ideal, of types, and of the passions broadly treated. *The Scarlet Letter* and *The Marble Faun,* Sylvester Judd's *Margaret,* and Stevenson's *Dr. Jekyll and Mr. Hyde* exemplify the form. Romances, he adds, partake of the nature of poems and are not to be judged by "the rules of criticism that apply to the novel." But the romanticistic novel seeks effect rather than truth, according to Howells: its motives are false, it is excessive in coloring and drawing, and it revels in "the extravagant, the unusual, and the bizarre." Two very great men, Dickens and Hugo, wrote books of this kind. Their success is due to readers, prevailing in number, who have childish imaginations and no self-knowledge.

As to the "outward shape of the inward life of the novel," Howells contends, the three principal kinds are the autobiographical, the biographical, and the historical. The first he holds to be the most perfect literary form after the drama, because the tale-teller is master of the situation and can report his first-person narrator's mind with authority. But the "I" narrator cannot go outside his own observations, the range of the form is narrow, and none of the greatest novels have been written in it except *Gil Blas,* though it is the form of *The Luck of Barry Lyndon, The Blithedale Romance,* and *David Copperfield.* (One wonders if Howells exempted, or forgot, *Adventures of Huckleberry Finn.*) The biographical novel, as Howells defines it, is the form in which the author's central figure, who must be of "paramount importance," reflects all the facts and feelings involved. Though he considers it "nearly as cramping as the autobiographical," he asserts that Henry James had used it in *Roderick Hudson* and has lately cast in it "work of really unimpeachable perfection." Here Howells is in effect predicting James's work of "the major phase." But the "great form," however impure and imperfect, he declares with much force and eloquence, is the "historical" form – the novel as if it were history. In it the novelist enters into the minds and hearts of his characters, invents speeches for them, gives their innermost thoughts and desires, and has their confidence in hours of passion or of remorse or even of death itself. He is a "universal intelligence" in this world. In spite of the contradictions, absurdities, improbabilities, and impossibilities inherent in the historical form, Howells prizes it as the "primal form of fiction" and a form of the future. "Think," he says, "of *Don Quixote,* of *Wilhelm Meister,* of *The Bride of Lammermoor,* of *I Promessi Sposi,* of *War and Peace,* of *Fathers and Sons,* of *Middlemarch,* of *Pendennis,* of *Bleak House,* of *Uncle Tom's Cabin,* of *The Scarlet Letter,* of *L'Assommoir,* of the *Grandissimes,* of *Princess Casamassima,* of *Far from the Madding Crowd,*" all masterpieces. The historical form may be "sprawling, splay-footed, gangling, proportionless and inchoate," he concludes, "but if it is true to the life which it can give no authority for seeming to know, it is full of beauty and symmetry."

The term "symmetry," drawn from Howells's study of art and architecture, introduces related ideas in his terms "perspective," "relation," and "proportion." All of them stem from his fondness for eighteenth-century English thought: concepts of rationality and control, measure and balance. The novel, he explained to Stephen Crane in an interview (1894), is "a perspective made for the benefit of people who have no true use of their eyes. The novel . . . adjusts the proportions. It preserves the balances." And again, it is "the business of the novel to picture the daily life . . . with an absolute and clear sense of proportion." What Howells means by these terms is presumably formal skill in representing norms of experience within the "microcosm" of the novel. Thus a storyteller like Maupassant, in Howells's view, often fails because he is "obsessed" with his own rather than with universal experience. Like Arnold, quoting Sophocles, Howells's goal is to "see life steadily and see it whole."

The effect that a novelist may achieve by representing his characters and their actions in "relation and proportion" is beauty and repose – terms not ordinarily associated with Howells's theory but central to his deepest intent. Repose, he explains (even as he admits he cannot define it), may arise from squalor or grief or agony in a piece of fiction; yet it is the quality that charms readers in every age, it is "the soul of beauty in all its forms." By repose, Howells may mean catharsis, "all passion spent," or he may mean the reader's rational pleasure in the inevitable working out of fictional logic. Perhaps he means both. As for truth, from truth to beauty is scarcely a step in Howells's theory of fiction. Realism is but the "truthful treatment of material," or the "truest possible picture of life." Truth, which is the only beauty, is "truth to human experience, and human experience is so manifold and so recondite, that no scheme can be too remote, too airy for the test."

If Howells seems vague in this definition of truth in the novel, he is far more precise in asserting what the business of the novelist is and what effect the masterwork of fiction has on its audience. The novelist, he asserts, had "better not aim to please," and he "had still better not aim to instruct." His story must be a work of art, outside the realms of polemics and ethics, and if his story does not tell, nothing in it tells. What, then, he asks, is the purpose of the novel, the chief intellectual stimulus and influence of the day, this "supreme literary form, the fine flower of the human story"? His answer is both shrewd and penetrating. Though *The Scarlet Letter* or *Romola* may at once instill the dread of falsehood, he says, the novel can affect readers only so far as it shall "charm their minds and win their hearts." It can do no good directly. "It shall not be the bread," Howells urges, "but the grain of wheat which must sprout and grow in the reader's soul and be harvested in his experience, and in the mills of the gods ground slowly perhaps many years before it shall duly nourish him." In his essay on Ibsen (1906), Howells restated his resolution of the ancient dispute over literature's instructing or pleasing. He said: "The great and dreadful delight of Ibsen is from his power of dispersing the conventional acceptations by which men live on easy terms with themselves, and obliging them to examine the grounds of their social and moral opinions." In the end of ends, Howells made this slow-working indirect power the prime tenet of his critical theory. He sought it in his own fiction. He achieved it in his best novels.

Selected Bibliography

A Bibliography of William Dean Howells by William M. Gibson and George Arms (New York: New York Public Library, 1948) lists Howells's primary writings. Jacob Blanck's *Bibliography of American Literature* (Vol. IV) adds certain contributions to books and pamphlets and refines upon issues. Titles given below are first editions; revised texts are not noted nor are translations. Much of Howells's writing is out of print, but *A Selected Edition of William Dean Howells* in 36 volumes, of which Edwin H. Cady is general editor, is forthcoming from Indiana University Press. The fullest list of criticism of Howells is the "Selected Bibliography" in Clara and Rudolf Kirk, eds., *William Dean Howells, Representative Selections* (New York: Hill and Wang, 1961). There are a number of current paperback reprints.

Works of William D. Howells

TRAVEL AND PLACE

Venetian Life. London: Trubner, 1866.
Italian Journeys. New York: Hurd and Houghton, 1867.
Three Villages. Boston: Osgood, 1884.
Tuscan Cities. Boston: Ticknor, 1886.
A Little Swiss Sojourn. New York: Harper, 1892.
London Films. New York: Harper, 1906.
Certain Delightful English Towns. New York: Harper, 1906.
Roman Holidays and Others. New York: Harper, 1908.
Seven English Cities. New York: Harper, 1909.
Familiar Spanish Travels. New York: Harper, 1913.

NOVELS

Their Wedding Journey. Boston: Osgood, 1872.
A Chance Acquaintance. Boston: Osgood, 1873.
A Foregone Conclusion. Boston: Osgood, 1875.
The Lady of the Aroostook. Boston: Houghton, Osgood, 1879.
The Undiscovered Country. Boston: Houghton, Mifflin, 1880.
Doctor Breen's Practice, a Novel. Boston: Osgood, 1881.
A Modern Instance, a Novel. Boston: Osgood, 1882.
A Woman's Reason, a Novel. Boston: Osgood, 1883.

The Rise of Silas Lapham. Boston: Ticknor, 1885.
Indian Summer. Boston: Ticknor, 1886.
The Minister's Charge, or The Apprenticeship of Lemuel Barker. Boston: Ticknor, 1887.
April Hopes. New York: Harper, 1888.
Annie Kilburn, a Novel. New York: Harper, 1889.
A Hazard of New Fortunes, a Novel. New York: Harper, 1890.
The Shadow of a Dream, a Story. New York: Harper, 1890.
An Imperative Duty, a Novel. New York: Harper, 1892.
The Quality of Mercy, a Novel. New York: Harper, 1892.
The World of Chance, a Novel. New York: Harper, 1893.
The Coast of Bohemia, a Novel. New York: Harper, 1893.
A Traveler from Altruria, Romance. New York: Harper, 1894.
The Day of Their Wedding, a Novel. New York: Harper, 1896.
The Landlord at Lion's Head, a Novel. New York: Harper, 1897.
An Open-Eyed Conspiracy, an Idyl of Saratoga. New York: Harper, 1897.
The Story of a Play, a Novel. New York: Harper, 1898.
Ragged Lady, a Novel. New York: Harper, 1899.
Their Silver Wedding Journey. New York: Harper, 1899.
The Kentons, a Novel. New York: Harper, 1902.
Letters Home. New York: Harper, 1903.
The Son of Royal Langbrith, a Novel. New York: Harper, 1904.
Miss Bellard's Inspiration, a Novel. New York: Harper, 1905.
Through the Eye of the Needle, a Romance. New York: Harper, 1907.
Fennel and Rue, a Novel. New York: Harper, 1908.
The Leatherwood God. New York: Century, 1916.
The Vacation of the Kelwyns, an Idyl of the Middle Eighteen-Seventies. New York: Harper, [1920].
Mrs. Farrell, a Novel. New York: Harper, [1921]. First serialized as "Private Theatricals" in the *Atlantic*, November 1875 to May 1876.

STORIES

Suburban Sketches. New York: Hurd and Houghton, 1871.
A Fearful Responsibility and Other Stories. Boston: Osgood, 1881.
A Day's Pleasure and Other Sketches. Boston: Houghton, Mifflin, 1881.
A Parting and a Meeting. New York: Harper, 1896.
A Pair of Patient Lovers. New York: Harper, 1901.
Questionable Shapes. New York: Harper, 1903.
Between the Dark and the Daylight, Romances. New York: Harper, 1907.
The Daughter of the Storage and Other Things in Prose and Verse. New York: Harper, [1916].

Selected Bibliography

POEMS AND PLAYS

Poems of Two Friends, with John J. Piatt. Columbus, Ohio: Follett, 1860.
No Love Lost, a Romance of Travel. New York: Putnam, 1869.
Poems. Boston: Osgood, 1873. Enlarged edition, Boston: Ticknor, 1886.
Stops of Various Quills. New York: Harper, 1895.
The Complete Plays of W. D. Howells, edited by Walter J. Meserve. New York: New York University Press, 1960. (Brings together all 36 plays.)

CRITICISM

Modern Italian Poets, Essays and Versions. New York: Harper, 1887.
Criticism and Fiction. New York: Harper, 1891.
My Literary Passions. New York: Harper, 1895.
Impressions and Experiences. New York: Harper, 1896.
"Novel-Writing and Novel-Reading, an Impersonal Explanation," in *Howells and James: A Double Billing,* edited by William M. Gibson and Leon Edel. New York: New York Public Library, 1958. (A lecture delivered in 1899.)
Heroines of Fiction. New York: Harper, 1901.
Literature and Life, Studies. New York: Harper, 1902.
Imaginary Interviews. New York: Harper, 1910.
The Seen and Unseen at Stratford-on-Avon, a Fantasy. New York: Harper, 1914.

CRITICAL INTRODUCTIONS

Prefaces to Contemporaries, edited by George Arms, William M. Gibson, and Frederic C. Marston, Jr. (Gainesville, Fla.: Scholars' Facsimiles and Reprints, 1957), collects 34 of Howells's introductions.

BIOGRAPHY

Lives and Speeches of Abraham Lincoln. Columbus, Ohio: Follett, Foster, 1860.
The Life and Character of Rutherford B. Hayes. Boston: Houghton, 1876.
"Meetings with King," in *Clarence King Memoirs.* New York: Putnam's, 1904.
My Mark Twain, Reminiscences and Criticisms. New York: Harper, 1910.

AUTOBIOGRAPHY AND REMINISCENCE

A Boy's Town. New York: Harper, 1890.
My Year in a Log Cabin. New York: Harper, 1893.
Literary Friends and Acquaintance, a Personal Retrospect of American Authorship. New York: Harper, 1900.
New Leaf Mills, a Chronicle. New York: Harper, 1913.
Years of My Youth. New York: Harper, [1916].

LETTERS

Life in Letters of William Dean Howells, edited by Mildred Howells. New York: Doubleday, Doran, 1928.

Mark Twain–Howells Letters . . . 1872–1910, edited by Henry Nash Smith and William M. Gibson. Cambridge, Mass.: Harvard University Press, 1960.

Biographical and Critical Studies

Bennett, George N. *William Dean Howells, the Development of a Novelist*. Norman: University of Oklahoma Press, 1959.

Brooks, Van Wyck. *Howells, His Life and World*. New York: Dutton, 1959.

Cady, Edwin H. *The Road to Realism, the Early Years, 1837–1885, of William Dean Howells* and *The Realist at War, the Mature Years, 1885–1920, of William Dean Howells*. Syracuse, N.Y.: Syracuse University Press, 1956, 1958.

——— and David L. Frazier, editors. *The War of the Critics over William Dean Howells*. Evanston, Ill.: Row, Peterson, 1962. (Sixty pieces, from excerpts to full articles, from 1860 to 1960.)

Carrington, George C., Jr. *The Immense Complex Drama: The World and Art of the Howells Novel*. Columbus: Ohio State University Press, [1966].

Carter, Everett. *Howells and the Age of Realism*. Philadelphia: Lippincott, [1954].

Cooke, Delmar G. *William Dean Howells*. New York: Dutton, 1922.

Eble, Kenneth E., editor. *Howells, a Century of Criticism*. Dallas, Texas: Southern Methodist University Press, 1962. (Twenty-eight essays.)

Firkins, Oscar W. *William Dean Howells*. Cambridge, Mass.: Harvard University Press, 1924.

Fryckstedt, Olov W. *In Quest of America, a Study of Howells' Early Development as a Novelist*. Cambridge, Mass.: Harvard University Press, 1958.

Hough, Robert L. *The Quiet Rebel, William Dean Howells as Social Commentator*. Lincoln: University of Nebraska Press, 1959.

Kirk, Clara M. *W. D. Howells, Traveler from Altruria, 1889–1894*. New Brunswick, N.J.: Rutgers University Press, 1962.

———. *W. D. Howells and Art in His Time*. New Brunswick, N.J.: Rutgers University Press, 1965.

——— and Rudolf Kirk. *William Dean Howells*. New York: Twayne, 1962.

McMurray, William. *The Literary Realism of William Dean Howells*. Carbondale: Southern Illinois University Press, 1967.

Woodress, James L., Jr. *Howells and Italy*. Durham, N.C.: Duke University Press, 1952.